How to Discuss 360 Feedback

The essential guide

Julie Cooper

Copyright Julie Cooper 2015

ISBN 978-0-9927587-4-5

Published by Spring Publishing, an imprint of Careertrain Publishing, Banbury, England

www.springpublishing.co.uk

hello@springpublishing.co.uk

How to Discuss 360 Feedback

The essential guide

Julie Cooper

Spring Publishing

Contents

TOPI – The Other Person Involved

The other person involved

Throughout this book, I refer to The Other Person Involved as Topi, which is much easier than saying feedback receiver, employee, coachee or any other not-quite-right word. You are you, the person you are talking to is Topi. Sometimes Topi is male, sometimes female.

Introduction

This book is for you if you have been asked to run one to one 360 feedback meetings. You may work in HR, learning and development, or be a coach or trainer. If you are new to the task or want to review your practice, pull up a chair.

Helping another person come to terms with their 360 feedback is a task that needs considerable skill, understanding and experience. Many people approach it with trepidation, and quite rightly so – it's an important job; it can be demanding and has the potential to go pear shaped.

On the other hand, done well, it is incredibly rewarding. You have the opportunity to support a fellow human come to terms with valuable information about themselves and plan how to reach their potential. For me, it doesn't get much better than that. Having said that, I do remember what it is like to dread the feedback meeting. What if Topi (Topi is an - acronym, meaning The Other Person Involved) gets angry? What if I can't help? What if they're in denial? What if neither of us can think of one single action point?

If you are new to 360 feedback, you may have a list of fears longer than that. The purpose of this book is to give you the tools and knowledge to approach the job with confidence. Hopefully your concerns will be addressed and you'll feel equipped to handle the discussion – or you might have identified your own skills gaps.

This is a practical guide, not an academic paper. You will need to look elsewhere if you want to study the science behind the tool. Also, this book won't tell you how to plan and implement 360 feedback within your organisation – that is another topic, and approaches vary considerably depending on what else is in place.

If you want a pragmatic approach to discussing 360 feedback that will tell you what good practice looks like with tips, hints and some troubleshooting of common concerns, you are in the right place.

1. What is 360 Feedback?

I'm 99% sure that you wouldn't be reading this if you didn't know, but just in case....

360 feedback is a mechanism for an individual to get feedback on their performance at work from a range of colleagues, typically their line manager, a few team mates, subordinates, possibly customers or people from other parts of the organisation. The '360' comes from the number of degrees in a full circle – the aim is to get feedback from all around the person.

Everyone involved is asked the same set of questions, and must score the individual accordingly. The questions may have been derived from your own competency framework (if you have one), or may have been bought off the shelf – there are some excellent products available, which match common job roles e.g. sales person, business leader, manager etc. Obviously it is important that the questions are relevant to the individuals' job role, or the resulting report will be meaningless.

Questionnaires are almost always completed online, although occasionally I do hear about some poor soul collating shedloads of info onto a spreadsheet manually (which really can't save money!). If your organisation is doing this, please do look at some of the online options available.

There are three key factors that should be considered when choosing an online 360 provider:

- **Ease of use**. There is no excuse for software that is clunky, inflexible, slow or hard to understand.

- **Quality of reports**. It should give you sufficient information to be incredibly useful, without drowning you in minutiae that will lead to overwhelm.
- **Robustness.** All software has blips occasionally. You need to know that the infrastructure is secure and well maintained, and that any issues or queries will be dealt with promptly and courteously.

The report presents all the information gained. Usually this is a combination of numbers, visual aids (e.g. bar charts or spider graphs) plus some free text, which are questions where the respondent can write a sentence rather than give a score. The free text answers are usually at the end of the report, and are along the lines of *"What should this person stop/start/continue doing?"*, or *"What does this person do well? What could they do differently?"* Often clues to why the scores are as they are lie here.

Make no mistake: a good, user friendly report will make the feedback meeting easier, but the quality of the meeting and the outcomes achieved rely far more on the skill of the facilitator – that's you!

The other person involved

2. Before You Say Yes

If you've been asked to take part in feedback meetings, it will help you enormously to understand the big picture in your organisation, rather than working on assumptions about why your company is going through the 360 feedback process. Topi may well ask questions around this to help him see things in context.

2.1 Why are we doing it?

Check your understanding with the person responsible for running the 360 project. It's likely that you'll discover that one or more of the following are true:

- The organisation wants to add more value to the annual appraisal cycle. Some companies use 360 feedback as part of or instead of the usual annual appraisal. Others use it as separate process at a different time of year.
- Those taking part are going through a management development programme and 360 feedback is either being used to help them focus on their development needs before the training, or it may be being used as a before and after measure too.
- The organisation wants to 'take the temperature' to see how its people are faring after a period of change.
- The company wants to facilitate development of a specific area or team to make them stronger for challenges ahead.

Make sure you know who to pass queries and concerns on to, it may be someone in house or an external consultant.

2.2 How are we doing it?

The Provider

Doing some homework on the provider that has been chosen will be useful. You might find articles or sample reports on their website, and possibly will have the chance to have a practice run yourself. I find this helpful – it is easier to build rapport if you have shared experience. I also like to know how the questions were chosen, so that I can reassure myself that they are fit for purpose, relating well to Topi's role.

Rollout

Also ask about rollout, so that you know who is involved. Topi often asks *"Why me?"* You can set his mind at rest if you understand the agenda and can explain the rationale. 'Top down' is a common approach, by department, team or job role are other possibilities. It may be a pilot, where your company is exploring the potential of 360 feedback, or trialling a new provider.

Resources

Unless you work for a small company, it is unlikely that you will all be doing 360 at the same time. If you do discover that hundreds are going through the process at the same time, dig a little deeper to make sure that it has been well planned and sufficient resources are in place to make it a success. Even with the ease of technology, it still takes time to answer questionnaires, print out reports, organise and carry out feedback meetings, which are all extra tasks to usual day-to-day roles.

The need for additional meeting space for feedback meetings is sometimes overlooked, so think ahead if this might be an issue for you.

Options

Before the 360 feedback starts, decisions will have been made that you need to be aware of. Confidentiality is one – who gets to see the report? Is it just you and Topi? HR? Line managers? A Project Leader? Trainer? This should be communicated to you in advance. Make sure you know what the deal is so that you can act appropriately, you could ruin trust between you if you assure Topi the report is confidential when it isn't.

Another way practice varies is when the report is issued. Some organisations let Topi see the report as soon as it is available. In this case, initial emotional responses to the feedback may well have passed by the time the feedback meeting comes along, Topi is likely to have reached some conclusions and have views on the way forward. He may have already started mapping out a development plan or made decisions.

Alternatively, the report may be held back so that you can be with Topi when he sees it for the first time. This means that you will be there to support Topi through those initial thoughts and reactions. As you have a different starting point, how you approach the meeting will not be the same.

There is no right or wrong here. You will find arguments for and against confidentiality and releasing reports in advance. The only caution I would add is that if you know there is a strong likelihood that Topi will be upset by the report, it makes sense to be with him to help him keep a sense of perspective. This is my opinion – but Topi might prefer to deal with it by himself!

3. The Aims of the 360 Feedback Meeting

The primary aims of a 360 feedback meeting are to:

- Help Topi interpret the report
- Understand and accept the results
- Identify his key strengths and development needs

Usually first steps towards goal setting and action planning also happen, although in one meeting you will be hard pressed to exactly define actions, as methods of addressing training needs have to be researched and agreed. Often a second meeting to firm up action plans takes place. Topi might be tasked to discuss and finalise goals with his line manager, or it may be left to Topi to decide what action to take. Of course, if no change or action takes place, the whole process will have been a waste of everyone's time.

Some organisations have a process for feeding outcomes and goals into existing development plans – you will need to find out if this is the case for you.

Your organisation might have other 'big picture' aims for the data generated. For example, they may intend to use it to analyse employee engagement, identify company wide or team strengths and weaknesses. This should not detract from helping Topi have a valuable personal development experience.

By the end of the feedback meeting:

- Topi has increased self awareness, and has learnt how colleagues perceive him

- Topi has had opportunity to reflect on the implications of the report
- Development points and topics for further investigation have been identified
- You will be satisfied that you have offered appropriate support and challenge to help Topi get maximum benefit from both the report and the feedback meeting

In a nutshell, going through 360 feedback should be enlightening, challenging, developmental and positive. Topi should be in a better place because of it.

4. What Skills do I Need to Run a Feedback Meeting?

You probably possess most of the skills you need, or I doubt you would have been asked to get involved. Still, an objective assessment of your own skills is needed, as is a clear understanding of your role. Let's clear up a potential confusion before we begin. We talk about you, the person sitting down with Topi and going through the report with him, as 'giving 360 feedback'. Actually, it's not you giving the feedback is it? It's those people who answered the questionnaire who provide the feedback. Your role is not mainly a 'telling' role. It's much more complex and subtle than that.

Receiving a 360 feedback report can provoke a range of responses, so you will need to be able to handle discussions sensitively and deal with any emotions that emerge. You also will support Topi in making sense of the information, understanding the implications and deciding what actions to take.

Before we take a look at the skills you will need, consider first about the impact you will have on Topi. Your body language (expression, stature, poise), tone of voice and choice of language will all affect how you are perceived. How do you want Topi to view you? What is appropriate? I'm guessing that your first thoughts will be around coming over as professional and approachable. Where you go from there may depend on your role. Do think it through and be honest with yourself; what do you do (consciously or subconsciously) when you don't want to engage with someone? Or you want them to hurry up/shut up/move on? If we understand and recognise the signs we send, we are in a better position to monitor ourselves and adjust our behaviour when we need to.

Here's a very typical example: let's say that the meeting is looking very likely to run over, you have no flexibility and another meeting booked straight afterwards. Your automatic reaction may be to speed up, talk faster, look at your watch, give shorter answers, and encourage Topi to skip sections. Think for a minute how that will seem to Topi. How would you feel if his shoes were on your feet? A 360 report can seem like a very big deal. Being rushed through the feedback meeting could make Topi feel that it's not important, that he isn't worth the time, that the organisation is only paying lip service to the process. Thinking in advance what you will do – and how you want to be perceived – in potential difficult scenarios will help you position yourself in the right way.

Let's get back to the skills you'll need. They are the type of skills you might learn on a counselling or coaching course such as:

- Contracting
- Active listening
- Questioning
- Explaining
- Challenging
- Exploring
- Goal setting
- Action planning
- Being person centred

A brief overview of these is given below to help you review your current level of skill. Some of them you may have picked up from your experience, others you may need to work on. Do be honest with yourself here, and get impartial feedback from others who understand these skills where you can. Reading this book will not plug your skills gaps, but identifying them is a good place to start. I've included some questions at the end of each skill to help you. I suggest for each one you:

- Rate yourself
- Ask what evidence you have to support the rating
- Think what it would take to improve your score

There are plenty of resources around that will give you greater depth in each area, so I'm not going to reinvent the wheel here. My aim is to make sure you have considered your own skills and encourage you to develop them further.

4.1 Contracting

This means agreeing together what will happen during the meeting. It is always worth checking what the other person expects from you, so that you can correct any misconceptions. It is also your opportunity to set Topi at rest, by explaining briefly what is going to happen. Hopefully, this process will begin before you sit down together – for example in an email inviting Topi to the meeting – so that you do not need to start from scratch every time.

Does this seem unnecessary? Many problems that arise during feedback meetings occur because expectations aren't aligned. What if Topi thinks you will have all the answers? Or have access to the training budget? Or expects you to relay the conversation to his boss? You both need to know what will happen regarding:

- Who will see the report
- What you are there to do
- How long the meeting will last
- What (if any) the next steps are
- Confidentiality
- Impartiality

Is there anything else to be included that is pertinent to your organisation or your role? If you have an agenda, it is best to disclose it.

It doesn't work well if you open the meeting by exchanging pleasantries and then launch into a monologue explaining all the above. You are aiming to encourage Topi to open up to you, so putting her in 'receiving' mode is likely to shut her down. Instead, give some thought to questions you can ask to establish what she already understands so that you can fill the gaps or put a different slant on things. Here are some examples:

"Topi, did you see the email that explains why we are meeting?"
"What do you expect to happen today, Topi?"
"What's your understanding of what we have to do today?

When both sides are happy that they are clear about why they are meeting and what needs to be done, you are ready to move on. More of that later.

Think!

* ★ *Have you ever set expectations for others before a meeting or training day? If so, how effective was it?*

* ★ *Have you ever experienced people having a different understanding of what was going to happen? What difference would it have made if contracting had been done properly?*

* ★ *In your context and your own language, what exactly would you say to Topi at the beginning of the meeting?*

4.2 Active listening

The quality of listening we need when we are carrying out 360 feedback meetings – or any other one to one discussion where we have a supporting role – is different to every day listening. It rarely comes naturally to us to give another person our full concentration, which is what active listening is. This means not just hearing the words, but also noticing tone, emotions and body language as well.

By giving Topi all your attention, there should be no space for you to be thinking about other things, or planning what you will say next – which is what we usually do when someone else is speaking. This means that there may be short silences while you choose how to respond. That's fine.

Active listening is a process that involves:

1. **Concentrating** on what Topi is saying, which includes observing visual clues such as body language and also reading between the lines.
2. **Processing** the information you receive and getting clarity by questioning and exploring where you are unsure.
3. **Choosing** how you wish to respond. *(Taken from Face to Face in the Workplace)*

You can see from this that active listening also involves speaking sometimes, as you may need to ask questions to understand or confirm what Topi is telling you.

First of all, let's look at what gets in the way of effective listening:

Internal distractions such as things on your mind, pressure you are under, stuff you are trying not to forget, to do lists, worries, thinking ahead to later meetings, headaches, tiredness, thirst...

External distractions such as interruptions, ringing phones, email alerts, machinery, other conversations, the pile of paperwork on your desk, background music...

It makes you wonder how we ever manage to listen to each other at all! Learning to be an active listener will help your one to one skills enormously. When a conversation is important, or it is a formal occasion such as a performance review, you will need this skill even more.

Think!

★ **What distracts you most from giving another person your full attention?**

★ **How can you get more experience of giving another person your undivided attention?**

★ **What questions would you ask to help you understand what Topi is saying?**

★ **Try listening to another person for two minutes without speaking.**

4.3 Questioning

Please don't assume that you have good questioning skills. Questioning is a really useful skill on many levels – and my opinion is that it is also a skill that is in major shortage in the workplace.

Most of us go into telling mode without considering questioning as an option, yet the truth is that skilful questioning can make Topi realise for herself what needs to be done. Think about it – if someone tells you what to do, you are likely to respond somewhere on the spectrum between compliance and resistance – but if it is your idea, you are much more likely to take ownership and have commitment to the task.

Another crucial issue is that if we don't ask questions, we act without having full understanding of the situation and context. This is how bad decisions are made – too often we are so result focused, that an ill thought action seems preferable to more exploration.

In the context of 360 feedback, effective questioning can achieve three key things:

1. Helping you and Topi to understand the whole picture and Topi's key issues, which can guide you in structuring your conversation.
2. Helping Topi to see things from other perspectives, thinking outside of her normal box and considering other viewpoints.
3. As I mentioned above, helping Topi to form her own conclusions about the scores and comments in the

360 report, in a well considered way, taking both logical and emotional aspects into account.

A skilled questioner will have a collection of questions to draw upon and will learn through experience what types get the best outcomes. Thinking through what you might ask in advance can help smooth the way. What could you ask to help you achieve each of the three things above?

Here are a few examples to start you off:

1. *"Can you tell me about your current situation?" "What is your top priority right now?" "What is going through your mind?" "How do you see your role developing?"*
2. *"What does your Manager see as your strengths?" "How does your personal style impact on your team?" "How do you think it feels to be managed by you?"*
3. *"What do you think this part of the report is telling you?" "What do you make of these scores?" "Looking at these comments, do you think any action is needed?"*

Of course, your meeting is not about being The Inquisition – Topi is not on trial here – so you need to make sure that you do not overdo your questions. Allow space for responding to Topi, and also remember that Topi may well need thinking time so short silences are okay. In fact, leaving pauses will often prompt Topi to say more. Don't jump in to fill them.

You'll also need to ask probing questions, to give you opportunity to dig beyond Topi's initial answer. You might use phrases like *"Tell me more about that..." "Can you give me a bit more detail?" "How did you reach that conclusion?"* And my favourite one: *"What makes you say that?"*

Types of questions to avoid

Too many 'Why's. Think of asking a child *"Why did you do that?"* There is nothing fundamentally wrong with 'why' questions, but they can come across as accusatory or overly challenging. If you've used one or two, try to avoid them for a while by rewording. You could say *"What led you to do that?"* instead.

Multiple questions. *"What do you make of those scores? Have you thought of action points? What will you do first?"* Slow down! Ask one question at a time.

Leading questions. This is about Topi, not you. Be careful to make sure that your questions neither reflect your own views *"That marketing team always make things difficult, don't they?"* Or your assumptions about Topi *"I bet you're tired of working nights, aren't you?"* It is hard enough for Topi to think through the issues, without you making it more difficult by introducing inaccurate hurdles for them to jump.

Think!

★ *Are there situations where you can practise asking exploring questions to help you get the full picture? Try to draw information out of people rather than telling them.*

★ *Be aware of the questions you currently use. What responses do you get?*

★ *Build up your own list of questions that you will find useful.*

4.4 Explaining

There may be things you need to explain to Topi, from why she was asked do the 360 exercise to how the report is laid out. Explaining is reasonably straightforward, but we've all had those times when we haven't quite grasped something because it hasn't been explained well.

Here are a few tips:

- Explain one thing at a time, and check that Topi has understood before moving on. For example, if you explain graphs, scores, competency frameworks and free text without drawing breath, Topi will have forgotten the first thing well before you get to the last. Allow some thinking time between sentences for Topi to digest what you have said.
- Never assume prior knowledge – always check. Building on existing knowledge is the key, so you need to establish what Topi already understands, and start from there. Asking *"Have I explained that clearly?"* can be better than asking *"Do you understand?"* which is rarely a good question as you may not get an honest answer. You are more likely to be able to assess understanding from their comments and questions, which is one reason for a good dialogue.
- On the other hand, if you start at the very beginning when Topi is already familiar with what you are explaining, you run the risk of sounding patronising, being irritating, and damaging the rapport between you with Topi switching off!
- Be aware of industry or role specific jargon and acronyms you use. They can interrupt the flow or

cause misunderstanding. While Topi is trying to remember what the RFDO is that you mentioned, she will miss what you are currently saying.

Think!

* *When did you last explain something? How do you know how well you were understood?*

* *When did someone last explain something to you? Could they have done anything differently to make it better for you?*

4.5 Challenging

Challenging does not mean being confrontational. It's not about a standoff between two sides. It is about helping another person to see things differently, usually when they are blinkered in some way. For example, it could be when they are:

- Responding irrationally to information
- Making assumptions without evidence
- Seeing things as only black and white
- Distorting the facts to fit their own view of the world
- Failing to own a problem or shortcoming
- Not recognising the consequences of their actions or behaviour
- Contradicting themselves or behaving inconsistently

It can feel difficult to address some of these issues, but what is the alternative? If you ignore them, you are doing Topi a disservice. She won't be able to move forward if she is not aware of the issues. One caveat: remember that your role is to help Topi make sense of the information and move forward, not to impose your view of what she should do. Be careful to be as impartial as you can.

So how do we challenge? If we take being confrontational out of the equation, we have other options open to us. One is to have an objective stance; you can use this to give information, pass on facts, or say what you see in the report if Topi is misreading it. You may feel a defensive response rise up if Topi shows a negative emotional one, but you don't need to be drawn into it. It is her issue, not yours.

More useful is the approach of being curious; trying to understand and get to the bottom of what is going on. In the One to One Toolkit (Cooper and Reynolds) we suggest using phrases like:

"I'm getting mixed messages from you. You say....but your actions are...."
"On one hand....but on the other hand..."
"You tell me... but I see something different..."

We have already mentioned probing questions, such as *"What makes you say that?"* which can be useful challenging tools. Here are a few other methods:

- Ask a direct question
- Give feedback on what you see. Often non verbal and tone of voice cues go unchallenged. *"You visibly tensed when I mentioned your manager. What is the issue?"*
- Hold up a mirror: reflect Topi's own words back to her. Often Topi can see how she is distorting things when she hears her own words fed back to her.
- Invite Topi to change her language. *"Is it that you can't do it, or you choose not to?"*

The next section on exploring may help with challenging too.

If you reach a stalemate you can use phrases like *"Let me leave it with you to think about"* and move on. Don't be discouraged if Topi seems to be immovable. Our natural response to being challenged, no matter how tactfully it is done, can be defensive. In my experience, Topi may well have second thoughts after the meeting and take on board the tough messages. Your job is not to change Topi's mind for her – only she can do that. Yours is to make sure she has the information she needs and the opportunity to process it effectively.

Think!

* *What situations do you see around the workplace where you would like to challenge someone?*

* *How could you go about it? What words would you use?*

* *What would your body language and tone need to be like?*

4.6 Exploring

We have already said that there is a danger in taking things at face value; sometimes we need to uncover more information to be able to do an effective job of making sense of a 360 report. But just how much exploring do we need to do? Sometimes it's just a quick verification of facts that is needed, at other times it is trying to get to the bottom of issues that are unclear.

Firstly, you don't have the time to do an in depth analysis of every little detail, so some prioritising will be necessary. We need to cut our cloth according to the resources and time available.

Another important factor to take into account is the difference in style between your natural inclination to dig deeply and Topi's. For example, if you are an introvert with a reflective style, you will be drawn to pondering thoroughly on one topic before moving on. If Topi is an extravert she is more likely to be interested in breadth than depth, and may want to flit between topics. The meeting is about helping Topi, so you may have to bend towards her style, but without compromising the purpose of your discussion. Of course, if you have similar natural inclinations, the job may seem easier but you might miss the depth you need – or get stuck down a very deep hole! Be aware of your personal approach and the impact it can have.

How do we explore effectively? What works for me is to have simple frameworks that encourage me to question or think from different perspectives, so that different viewpoints and facts are uncovered. I visualise it as walking around a problem – another way of capitalising on the idea of 360 degrees!

Here are a few I use. If they are not familiar to you, I suggest that you think of a problem, and then think how you could frame a question or two around each aspect.

De Bono's Six Hats

This is a lovely framework, useful in so many contexts. If Topi is inclined to be 'stuck' in one type of thinking – for example emotional or negative – it will prompt you to move him on. There is no right or wrong order to use the hats in. It makes sense to finish with blue, although it can be used at other points to summarise thinking so far. Often they make a good checklist; you can mentally tick off the areas you have covered and see what is left. The trick is to postpone decision making until all six have been considered.

Let's take a hypothetical example of Topi complaining that he can't reach targets because of the high staff turnover in his team. Below are examples of questions you could ask to help you both get to grips with the situation:

Virgin White: Pure facts, figures and information

"How many team members have left this year?"
"What reasons do they give for leaving?"
"How long does it take to recruit a new person?"

Seeing Red: Emotions and feelings, also hunch and intuition

"How does the situation make you feel?"
"What is your hunch about the real reason they leave?"
"How does the turnover affect the team spirit?"

Devil's Advocate Black: Problems and difficulties, negative judgements, why it will not work

"What problems does staff turnover cause?"
"How much is this costing the company?"
"What is the impact on you personally?"

Sunshine Yellow: Positive and constructive, optimism, opportunities

"What are the benefits of having fresh blood in the team?"
"How can you maximise the opportunity of having new people?"
"What positive difference would a well established team make?"

Fertile Green: Creative, new ideas springing from lateral thinking, provocation

"What ideas do you have for reducing turnover?"
"What haven't you tried yet?"
"What would change the situation?"

Cool Control Blue: Overview, summaries and conclusions, orchestra conductor, thinking about thinking

"What is your assessment of the problem?"
"Taking everything into account, what are your thoughts about what needs to happen next?"
"How would you summarise the situation?"
                    ("Six Thinking Hats" Edward de Bono 1985)

NLP Perceptual Positions

This sounds more complicated than it is. There are three positions in this model. Firstly, there is Topi's position. How does she see the current situation? Once Topi has had opportunity to state her views and you have established her thoughts, move to the second position – the other party involved.

In this example above, it would be her team members, so you would ask Topi questions around how she thinks her team members view the situation. How does it affect them? What are their concerns? Asking Topi what it is like to be in another person's shoes is always useful for shifting perception. If this is something Topi has considered little before, you may need to have a few gentle questions up your sleeve to help her explore it.

Thirdly is the perception of those not involved in the scenario, an outsider looking in. In the context of 360 feedback, this might be another department within the organisation. What does Topi think they see when they look at the high turnover in her team? What assumptions might they make?

This gives Topi the opportunity to see things through new eyes and broaden her own perception – it is a powerful tool.

Offa's Agenda

Topi will arrive with an agenda of some kind – it will be made up of presenting issues, thoughts and concerns about what will happen next. There is always a danger in attempting to help her without realising the significance, depth or importance of aspects of her story.

Offa's Agenda is a simple model that breaks down the components we need to explore to make sure we discover, to the best of our ability, a realistic understanding of Topi's position. If you can remember the acronym, you have a framework for exploring with her. Has Topi explained the facts and her feelings? Can you help her separate out assumption and opinion?

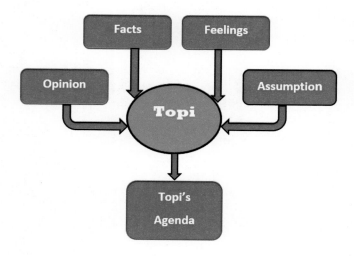

In our example above, Topi may say that she uses a recruitment agency instead of the in house HR department because they are useless and inefficient. What is she basing her opinion on? Is she making assumptions based on limited information? You can sometimes alter perception by giving information, which in this scenario may be talking about how recruitment has been successful in other departments.

We are all entitled to have an opinion, but it's important that we shed light so that Topi realises if she is basing her opinion on unsound criteria. It takes skill to do this without either party becoming defensive, which can easily happen if someone challenges what we believe to be true.

The Feeling category is interesting too, as it requires us to suspend our own thoughts on the emotions we would expect Topi to attach to parts of her story. Most of the time we can guess the range of feelings that are likely to be attached to events, e.g. we are nervous before interviews, happy to be promoted etc, but now and then you will find someone who does not present the emotions you would expect. We need to get a handle on how Topi feels – and the depth of the feelings – to be able to adjust the discussion to best meet her needs. I've dealt with clients that have felt totally devastated by the threat of redundancy, while others take it in their stride or positively rejoice that freedom is coming. Never assume!
(Adapted from the One to One Toolkit, Cooper and Reynolds)

Why are you asking me these questions?

Lastly, it's worth bearing in mind that Topi can't see inside your head. You may be merrily asking questions to cover all six hats or all three perceptual positions, but Topi won't know that. In the interests of transparency and good faith, it is good practice now and then to say *"I am asking you this because…."*.

You might even want to share the model you are using with Topi.

Think!

* *Practise using some of these tools to get acquainted with them.*

* *Next time you see someone jumping into action, ask a few exploring questions to ascertain if they've thought it through.*

4.7 Goal setting

I'm not going to say too much here, because most of us are well versed in SMART goals and have mechanisms in house to record them. If you don't have, do give it some thought in advance so that you have a way of capturing them.

Goal setting should be motivating and inspiring, causing us to be energised, raring to go and do whatever it takes... Often they are not, especially if we've worked in an organisation hide bound in administration where our 'goals' are bestowed upon us from above with minimal input from us.

Yes, you may need to feed the outcomes of your 360 feedback meetings into the systems your organisation has in place, but your focus on this should be secondary. My suggestion is that you park 'what needs to be done' and focus firstly on helping Topi identify goals that she really, really can see the benefit of achieving.

Also, goal setting may need to be tentative. Depending on how new the ideas for goals are, Topi may need to live with them for a few days to let her thoughts process them properly. Far better to have tentative actions that are firmed up effectively than definite goals that quickly crumble and fall by the wayside.

Having parked the paperwork, what is it we need to do? Here are my top tips:

- Look for the spark. Throughout your meeting, observe Topi's reactions. Note strength of feelings, whether it is body language giving you clues, or the way she speaks. Check out your observations. *"You seem very enthusiastic about restructuring the department. Have I got that right?" "You slumped visibly when I mentioned staff turnover. Is this a real concern for you?"* You may help Topi clarify her own feelings by doing this. Ultimately, you are getting confirmation about the things that matter, so that you can check that goals set are in the right ball park. You would expect that Topi is already aware of these issues, but sometimes new realisation dawns and Topi surprises herself!

- Here, more than ever, it is important that you let Topi take ownership and lead the way. Ask her what she sees as important moving forward. Use her language. Ask her what action she wants to take. Start with general questions and then drill down. *"So what could you do about that? What would it take?"*

- Do a rough cost/benefit analysis for each potential goal. Ask Topi what would be better/different if the goal were achieved. Get as much detail as you can. *"Is there anything else? Are there any other benefits?"* You'll soon be able to tell if Topi buys in to the idea. From there you can move to *"What would it take to achieve that?"* to help Topi decide if it is worth the effort.

- Don't let Topi get carried away, setting a zillion goals – you would be setting her up for failure. If she identifies many, ask her to prioritise her top three. Apply common sense here. If a goal or two are fairly achievable quick wins, it's fine to have more than three. Overload is a personal concept!

- On the other hand, if goals are not stretching in some way, they are unlikely to be motivational and inertia soon sets in. Sometimes Topi deliberately plans very small goals because she thinks she already has enough to do. She may have a point. If she has big, well thought out goals already, don't feel that you have to make her generate new ones. If she's just jaded or evasive, it's back to looking for the spark.

Think!

* **Do you know what your own goals are? How can you help someone else if you haven't done it for yourself?**

* **How have you felt about goals set in the past? Have you seen them through?**

* **What would make a goal motivating for you?**

4.8 Action planning

You may not be able to flesh out action plans properly – it's a lot to ask for in one meeting, but do record ideas and broad aims as you go so that they are not lost. If you are able to have a follow up meeting it can help enormously. In between meetings, Topi can check out resources available, the support the company will give her, different ways of learning etc.

You might need to help her weigh up the pros and cons of different approaches and be realistic about the time and energy she can contribute. It is also wise to be a little circumspect about the support she can expect from the organisation that employs her. Ultimately, we are all responsible for our own development. I've seen many people come up with great ideas for training they feel they should have, only to feel let down when the company says they can't release them. Don't rely on someone else's budget.

We've said that goal setting needs to be in Topi's language and to her agenda to get her full commitment. Similarly, action plans need to be created in a way that Topi can identify with and use happily. You might need to use in house forms. If so, it's worth having the discussion with Topi to find out what would work best for her. She may use scheduling or planning tools that could incorporate her actions, which would be far more useful to her than a company form that is filed and never revisited.

Think!

* **What obstacles stop people completing action plans?**

* **How can you construct an action plan so that it is useful and motivating?**

* **How can you tell the difference between a healthy, stretching action point and a step too far?**

4.9 The person centred approach

Lastly – and not to be overlooked – you need to consider your own motives. The most effective feedback meetings are person centred, i.e. they focus on helping Topi make sense of the report and deciding what actions to take, rather than trying to lead her down a particular path. The facilitator is an impartial, supportive helper who has no specific agenda. In reality this is not always easy to achieve, but do be aware of your own agenda so that you can monitor its impact on your meeting.

Some organisations like to use line managers to give feedback. Managers will often have clear ideas of what they want their staff to do in the future, which may be at odds with how Topi sees her career developing. Discussing a 360 report with your manager is a good thing to do, but it may be best done as a later activity, rather than as the initial feedback meeting. This gives Topi the space to come to terms with the report and decide how and what they want to share with her manager.

The other person involved

Think!

⭐ **When you are with different people, what are your own motives?**

⭐ **Have you any experience of parking your own motives to focus on another person? Where could you practise this?**

4.10 Are you good to go?

Hopefully you will have given your own skills an honest appraisal, and now have a fair idea how prepared you are to carry out the job in hand. In addition, be aware that some of the comments or scores may touch on difficult issues, or come as bad news to Topi, for example if she discovers that she is not as well respected as she thought. It's not common for Topi to get angry or upset, but it does happen sometimes. It is important that you feel confident to cope with situations like these, as well as the process of going through a report. If you have any doubts, do something about it before you need to conduct a live meeting. Here are some ideas:

- Find a more experienced colleague who is prepared to mentor or train you
- Ask if you can shadow other colleagues to see them in action
- Do your own research and study around your skills gaps
- Take a clear breakdown of where you see your skills gaps to your L&D department to see if they can help
- Set up an in house forum where everyone involved can share good practice

If you still feel that conducting a 360 feedback meeting is outside your competence, talk to your Project Manager and ask for someone else to take the role until you feel your skills are up to scratch.

5. Before the Meeting

You'll probably prefer to look at the 360 report ahead of the meeting so that you feel well prepared before you sit down with Topi. As well as familiarising yourself with the style and layout so that you can easily find your way around it, you can also:

- Identify the main themes that arise. There may be clues across the competences
- Make a note of any inconsistencies or mixed messages to be explored
- Identify perceived strengths
- Gather some ideas about potential areas for development

This isn't a comprehensive list – 360 reports have different content, so to some degree you are guided by the provider you have chosen.

Don't rush to get your thoughts down. Sometimes you'll get towards the end of the report and find information that contradicts something you've seen earlier. Instead, read the whole report and let the big picture sink in before you try to draw conclusions. Once I've read a report, I usually flick back and forth between the sections to see how different sections relate to each other, or to look for evidence (or the opposite) of a theme I think I see.

Try not to get bogged down in the detail along the way. If you start by trying to take on board every detail, it's highly likely that you won't be able to see the wood for the trees because you will have too much data to absorb and no framework to arrange it in your brain. If you look across sections for themes, strengths, development points etc. first, you might find it easier as you'll have hooks to hang your thoughts on. This is how I prefer to work; your learning style may lead you to take a different approach and that's fine.

A good report will be reasonably straightforward to interpret. If, once you have acclimatised yourself to the layout and contents of the report, you are struggling with overload or insufficient information, it may be worth comparing other providers and making recommendations to your project manager.

A word of warning here: an easy mistake to make at this point is to be subconsciously reacting to the report as if it were yours, i.e. what would you do if you got this report? What would you be pleased about? What goals would you want to set yourself as a result of the feedback?

This is dangerous because it's not about you. Topi may have a different point of view, different priorities – and he definitely knows more about the context that the scores and remarks come from than you do. You might think that it is safe to assume that anyone would be happy with good feedback, and unhappy with negative comments, but that is an assumption and not always the case. Take for example Keith, who I was dreading walking through the door. He had one of the most difficult 360 reports I have ever seen, littered with low scores and negative comments. He came into the room, shook my hand, and said *"It's ok. I know everyone hates me"* – and then continued to be pleasant, pragmatic and focused throughout our time together.

Of course you are allowed to have an opinion – but you don't need to push it onto Topi. Instead, view the report rationally, and be aware of your own 'buttons' – the items that provoke a response in you because of who you are – and try to put them to one side.

How you physically review the report depends on how you like to work. I tend to print off a second copy of the report I can scribble on, usually in pencil, so that I can make light marks if I want to, and also have pen and paper to hand to note down thoughts or questions along the way. You might prefer to work on a PC. Bear in mind that whatever you take into the meeting with you could distract or influence Topi. Imagine how he will react if he can see a big asterisk or question mark next to a score; it is bound to interrupt his train of thought.

Once you've got to grips with the report you can:

- Prepare some questions or topics for discussions based on the themes the report reveals.

- Think through possible reactions to potentially upsetting information. How might Topi respond? How else might he respond? For each possible reaction, think through how you will handle it.

- If it is your company's policy to give the report to Topi in advance of the meeting (some don't, choosing instead for Topi to see it for the first time at the meeting), check in advance that he has it and has read it, to save you wasting time.

- Remember this meeting is about Topi's development, not what you think he should do. What steps can you take to ensure you remain impartial and supportive?

Lastly, don't forget the practicalities. Your discussion with Topi will require concentration from both of you, so make sure that you have access to an appropriate environment. You will need a quiet, comfortable room where there will be no interruptions. I usually allow an hour and a half to two hours for each feedback meeting.

Don't do too many feedback sessions on top of each other. If you have to do them back to back, allow yourself at least a coffee break between sessions so that you have time to make any notes from one session, for example, to jot down any follow up actions you said you would do, or how you agreed you would stay in touch.

You also need to mentally 'put down' Topi, to clear your mind before the next Topi comes through the door. We all deserve to be treated as the unique individuals that we are. This becomes difficult if you have a stream of people entering the room, all holding a report with an identical format. They might even have similar content, reflecting the company they work for or job role. If you've tried interviewing several candidates for jobs in quick succession, you'll understand what I mean. Our brains start to blur the edges between the Topis, assuming similarities that actually are not there, or muddling the contents of the reports. It takes a deliberate, conscious act to clear your mind and give the next Topi a fresh start.

6. During the Meeting

Your role during the meeting is to focus your attention on being there for Topi as together you review his 360 report. This means helping him to keep things in perspective and be constructive, also assisting him in identifying the action points that will have most impact.

6.1 Is the room fit?

Arrive in good time so that you can make sure the room is appropriate and fit for purpose. I've been put in a room during winter that hasn't been used for a few days that was an icebox, a room that had housed a student event and still had food debris and litter everywhere, been directed to a locked room where the key holder is nowhere to be found... Of course, all of these scenarios are easily surmountable given a little time, but become frustrating spoilers if you turn up on the dot expecting everything to be in order.

6.2 Are we ready to go?

Your aim in these first few minutes before you get down to business is to make sure that Topi is in the right frame of mind to have a meaningful discussion. You'll need to use your judgement here. Some people are anxious to dive straight in, others won't concentrate until they've got comfortable with you, which means they use the time spent mentioning the weather or their journey as a way of 'tuning in' to you. The pleasantries you'll exchange to break the ice may depend on how well you know Topi.

Do take a moment to check out Topi's demeanour as it will give you clues to his mood. It is natural for some people to be a bit anxious when facing a 360 report for the first time, they usually settle into it once they understand what is going to happen and begin to see the results.

If you spot anything worrying beyond this, my approach would be to deal with it openly up front. *"You seem very tense, Topi. Are you just concerned about your 360 report, or is there anything else on your mind?"* You may be opening a can of worms, or may not be equipped to deal with the issue that emerges. You don't need to get drawn into Topi's problems beyond acknowledging them. The bottom line is that you need to know whether it is a wise idea to carry on with the meeting or not. You can say something like *"I can see you have a lot on your plate. Will you be able to focus on your report today?"* Or you can state your case more strongly: *"I can see you have a lot going on at the moment, but it would be quite tricky to reschedule. Shall I explain what we need to do today, so that you can decide if you are able to continue?"* Your time is as valuable as Topi's, so both need taking into account.

In my experience, no one has ever elected to not continue – I guess they all know they will need to face the report sometime. Most initial negative responses seem to be about venting frustrations about having yet another thing to deal with, or being scared of a damning report. If you position the meeting as a two way discussion where you are listening and responding to Topi, rather than just being in 'telling' mode and dumping information on him, you should be able to successfully overcome awkward beginnings.

6.3 Setting the agenda

Your task here is to explain to Topi what will happen during the meeting, so that he feels reassured and is willing to participate. We've touched on this in 'Contracting' in the skills section above, so do go back and take a look if you skipped that section. You will need to:

- Explain your role as a facilitator and what you hope will be achieved by the end of the meeting. This is usually that Topi understands the feedback, has had opportunity to explore it and talk it over, and has begun to form ideas for action he will take as a result of it
- Ask Topi if this is what he expected, so that you can correct any misunderstandings
- Tell Topi how long the meeting will last, what is confidential and who will see the report
- Ask Topi if he has any questions or concerns before you begin

If the 360 feedback is linked to other processes you have in your organisation, such as training plans or appraisal, make sure you have a thorough understanding of what Topi needs to do, so that you can advise him if you need to, plus you will need to check Topi's awareness of these processes as part of setting the agenda.

6.4 Work through the report

To do this well, you will need to find out what is going on around Topi at work so that you have a context and know what is important to him. This will help you understand his initial response to the report and why he chooses areas he would like to concentrate on. At this stage, you will have more questions than answers. Be aware that any conclusions you have drawn by reading the report in advance may seem different once you have heard Topi's context and explanation, so be prepared to change your view. Express all of your own thoughts tentatively.

When you are working your way through the report, you are treading a fine line between providing a structure for Topi to follow and letting him take the lead. Usually it is best to start with the overview; most reports have some kind of summary at the beginning. Sometimes they are written, more often than not they are some type of visual representation, such as bar charts or spider diagrams designed to make the data more accessible. Bear in mind here that we have different learning styles and experience. Some people can't cope with a sea of numbers, others like nothing better than seeing their world on a spreadsheet. I've had clients with high levels of mathematical and analytical ability who have been completely thrown when data is presented in an unfamiliar way. Take some time to make sure Topi is grasping the information.

After you have looked at the overview, you can either go through the sections in the order they appear, or let Topi choose what he wants to discuss first. Sometimes Topi has a bee in his bonnet about a particular issue; far better to let him get it out of his system and deal with it than let him stew and be distracted, waiting for it to come up.

Another thing to bear in mind is that your approach will be slightly different depending on whether or not Topi has seen the report in advance. The advantages of Topi seeing it in advance are that you probably won't have to deal with any immediate emotional responses he had to it, and if he has taken the contents on board you are likely to get further with action planning because he has had time to think. On the other hand, sometimes Topi doesn't do a great job of reading the report, perhaps just focusing on the negatives, or skewing information. If this happens, you will need to gently guide him towards taking a more balanced view.

The advantage of Topi seeing it for the first time at the meeting is that he will have someone to talk to and help him keep a good sense of perspective right from the start. The downside, of course, is that you may have the initial emotional responses to deal with, and it can take longer to talk through the sections as it is all new to Topi.

6.5 Be alert to Topi's reactions

Part of the skill in facilitating a 360 feedback meeting is picking up signals from Topi, so that you can respond to them. We're talking about both verbal and non verbal language here. It's easy to get caught up in 'what bit comes next', but this should not be just an administrative exercise.

Is Topi picking up themes and linking items? Is he being realistic, over dramatising, or being dismissive? Is he withdrawing in certain areas, or lighting up in others? Look for the clues, and ask Topi to confirm whether your interpretation is right *"You don't seem too concerned about this...am I right?"* Guide him and mildly challenge where you need to.

6.6 Ask Topi to summarise his learning and thoughts

This is the surest way of discovering what Topi has taken on board and the direction he is heading. Summarising can be very useful; in addition to helping you understand where Topi is at, it can give Topi clarity too, as he puts his thoughts into words. It's fine to allow space here. It can be a big ask, so leaving a few moments silence for Topi to arrange his ideas can be helpful. You can also use summarising to mark the end of one part of the report before you move on to the next.

6.7 Flesh out the action points as far as possible

We've mentioned action planning above in the skills section. Let me just reiterate that it needs to be done in a way that works for Topi, or the actions just won't happen. We also said that it's very likely that Topi will need to go away and research the best ways of reaching his goals. There are many ways to learn a new skill, so time is needed to weigh up which method is best given Topi's situation, resources and learning style. This can mean that any action plan you draw up is tentative.

One danger is that either one of you will want to commit the action points to paper or screen just to get the job completed. Many of us are trained by busy working environments to get things done; another factor (which you'll know if you've ever done a Myers Briggs questionnaire) is that some of us have the type of personality that likes completion and struggles with tasks being half finished. Firstly, be aware if you see this happening. One approach that can help is to put in a date for completion *"Shall we say that you will email the finished action plan by the 20th?"* so that Topi can see the finished task on the horizon.

You might also need to help Topi to be realistic about the time and energy he has available too. Sometime he gets carried away with all the things he could do. If an action plan is over ambitious, it could set Topi up for failure, so do ask the questions around how he will achieve his goals. A process for revisiting them and amending if needs arise is helpful too.

6.8 End the meeting on a positive note

A 360 feedback meeting may be a place for serious conversations, but it should not leave Topi in a negative frame of mind. At the end of the meeting, ask Topi to recap his thoughts and ask how he is feeling. Many of us have an inclination to dwell on the negative, so try to make sure Topi has a balanced view and does not forget his strengths. Even in the worst case scenario, Topi still has the opportunity to change things for the better.

6.9 A few more tips on managing the meeting

Here are a few more pointers to help you have a productive session:

- Have a repertoire of coaching style questions you can use to get to the heart of the matter, e.g. *"What would you like to be different?" "Where do you want to be?" "How could you reach your goals?" "What steps do you need to take first?"* There are many lists of coaching questions available online. Have a browse, and pick out those you think may be valuable in the context of 360 feedback, and those that you can imagine yourself using, i.e. language you are comfortable with.

- Manage the time effectively, and revisit and adjust the agreed priorities if you need to. *"It seems as if this conversation is proving worthwhile to you, but we are in danger of not getting through the whole report in the time we have. Would you rather move on, or stay on this topic?"*

- When considering action points do discuss what support may be necessary, and any potential obstacles there may be to be overcome. How will progress be reviewed? Who will he be accountable to? This will help Topi plan realistically.

- It's possible that Topi has issues that you cannot deal with, that are outside of your skills and experience. Be honest with him. You can acknowledge the issue, you can even offer to find out who would be able to help. Don't leave Topi in the lurch, or fob him off with a name who might be able to help – or might not. Check in with him to make sure he has been able to access the support he needs.

The other person involved

7. After the meeting

Like any skill, conducting a 360 feedback meeting well can be developed, but it will only happen if you are prepared to learn. We mentioned some ways of developing your skills above. Another excellent way is to reflect on your own performance. Most professionals that work one to one take the time to reflect on their practice so that they can continue to hone their skills.

Ask yourself questions like:

- How successful was the meeting, and why?
- Did you meet the aims you set at the beginning?
- Is there anything you could have done differently?
- Is there anything you missed out?
- How could you do it better next time?
- Did Topi leave in a constructive, motivated frame of mind?
- Was Topi clear on next steps?

Many practitioners keep a reflective diary to record their progress. You can also make yourself an action plan and find yourself a buddy – someone else delivering feedback meetings – to share reflections with.

Besides developing yourself, there is also the organisational perspective to consider. If you found any sticking points along the way, such as unsuitable rooms, reports not being read or people complaining about the software, do give your feedback to whoever is organising the 360 process in your company.

8. Troubleshooting

Many 360 reports have aspects that may not be easy for Topi to take on board. Before we look at some of the common challenges, there are a few important things to bear in mind.

Is it Topi?

Remember that 360 feedback is people's perception based on their experience of Topi. This is not the same as fact. Exploring why others see Topi as they do is a worthwhile discussion in most tricky areas. Often discussions end up being about behavioural style rather than job competence. Sometimes other people are basing their scores on solid information; for example, a colleague may know for certain that Topi always gets her monthly figures done on time so may confidently score her highly on areas around conscientiousness and meeting deadlines. Another colleague may not have direct experience of Topi's output, but might see Topi in meetings, speaking to clients or around the office. If she sees Topi flustered, dithering or apparently wasting time, her perception may be that Topi is not that conscientious – the 'face' that Topi shows to others might vary.

Supporting Topi to rationally separate facts from perception can be challenging but is necessary. Topi will need to think carefully about how she presents herself in different scenarios, and whether her behaviour helps or hinders others to understand how she carries out her role. You might use questions like:

"What might your colleagues be basing their scores on?"

"Can you think of any aspects of your behaviour that might be interpreted in this way?"

"When do you think colleagues might see you in this light?"

"Are there times when your behaviour might not reflect your competence?"

"How do you react when X happens? How could your colleagues interpret that?"

Your role here is to help Topi come to terms with the feedback, and evaluate it analytically, looking for clues within herself to help her understand it. There might be silences, there may be uncomfortable moments while Topi has to reassess her actions. The changes in her thinking that emerge are the essence of 360 feedback, so don't avoid or rush this part of the process. If Topi genuinely can't understand why others perceive her as they do, it may be an action point for her to go away and do some further exploration, which could involve talking to colleagues and gathering more feedback until the picture becomes clear.

Is it the report?

If Topi is having real difficulty getting meaningful feedback from the report, it may be that the questions went out to respondents that weren't really appropriate for Topi's role. Some 360 feedback systems are more flexible than others allowing them to be tailored to specific needs, others are very generic, making it difficult to match them accurately to requirements.

Sometimes organisations will choose the same questionnaire for a group of people so that it is easy to compare results, but there can be snags with this approach. Here's an example: A company chooses to put all staff at the same senior level through the same questionnaire, which is aimed at Business Leaders. The questions assume that staff at that level have teams beneath them, and many questions are around people management. One person though, is an industry specialist and has a senior position but directly manages no one (an increasingly common scenario). This makes it difficult for her colleagues to answer the questions in a meaningful way – they may skip many, or just plump for the middle ground. The report can only reflect the answers, so is likely to have limited usefulness.

If Topi is struggling with the report, try going back to asking her about her role to check whether the competences in the report are a reasonable match.

Is it the respondents?

At some point, someone will have selected the colleagues to respond to the report. Often this is Topi, sometimes in collaboration with her manager, sometimes they are selected for Topi. Of course this is another area where the variables can have an impact. A good handful of respondents from a variety of sources is ideal; if there are only two or three you may not get a comprehensive picture and there is less chance that they will corroborate each other's views.

A bigger issue is that occasionally Topi will try to select respondents to skew the results. She might just choose her mates in an attempt to get a positive report, or she might think she knows what those around her think, so she casts her net wider and chooses people who may not know her so well. This may be done with the best of intentions, but it is possible that the upshot is that responses are based on little knowledge.

Once you've checked that the questionnaire reflected Topi's role well, ask her about the respondents so that you can help her judge how relevant their observations may be.

8.1 What do I do when Topi has a higher opinion of herself than others do?

Often this comes as a bit of a shock to Topi, so the first thing to do is allow her space to come to terms with it. Usually Topi is intelligent enough to work out the implications for herself. In your role as facilitator, you may need to support her, perhaps by helping her keep focus, or stopping her over dramatising.

Topi may have an emotional response at first, blaming the report, the process or the people involved. You can acknowledge her feelings without agreeing with what she is saying. There could be a number of reasons why this happens in a report, there are three obvious ones which Topi usually grasps fairly quickly:

- She is not performing as well as she thought she was.
- Topi has not fully understood what is expected of her. She is measuring herself against lower standards than others.
- Her achievements are not apparent to others – she is not presenting herself or her work in such a way that others see her capabilities.

All of these scenarios are likely to damage Topi's confidence so question her sensitively.

You'll want to discuss how she can get a more accurate understanding of what average, good and great look like in her role. There are often clues in the report – perhaps in the free text questions (where respondents write sentences rather than choosing a score) that give Topi an indication of where and how she is overestimating her ability, or underestimating what is expected in the role. If there aren't, you can help her prepare for a frank discussion with her line manager about the difference in perceptions.

If Topi feels that others just aren't seeing the value in the work she does – and this is quite common – you can have a conversation around how she can become her own PR agent. She may need to explore new ways of making her work more visible, or showing how her output contributes to company goals.

Either way, Topi has some homework to do and it may take her a while to come to terms with things not being as great as she thought they were. There is a danger here that Topi will start catastrophising and over reacting. Help her to keep a sense of perspective. If others say she is okay at her job – well, that's okay. If they say she is less than okay at her job, here is her opportunity to roll up her shirtsleeves and start fixing it.

8.2 What do I do when Topi has a lower opinion of herself than others do?

This is an interesting one. Some of the time you will discover that Topi deliberately marked herself down to avoid the embarrassment of a report that portrays her as big headed. This is quite straightforward; Topi is delighted to see that others have scored her more highly than she scored herself and her confidence improves.

It is less straightforward when Topi has genuine doubts about her ability. You can explore the reasons for this. They may include:

- She is new to the role and hasn't gained confidence yet
- Her line manager gives her little support or feedback, so she feels she has little clue about how she is doing
- There was an incident where things went badly around the time she completed the questionnaire, which knocked her confidence and affected how she scored herself
- There is so much change going on, Topi feels she is not on top of the situation but this is not apparent to others
- She has a natural tendency to put herself down, and does this in all walks of life

Your conversation can explore why Topi has a lower opinion of her competence, to try to uncover the reasons. It can be very rewarding to ask questions like *"What is it that others see that cause them to score you more highly?"* because it makes Topi articulate the positive. Once you have uncovered what is going on, you can help Topi think about development points that will take her in the right direction.

8.3 What do I do when everything is just average?

I think this is one of the hardest types of report to deal with. There is nothing standing out to home in on, no obvious areas to begin the discussion. Going through section after section can seem like Groundhog Day... Be careful here that you don't pass on your own thoughts, make sure that you use open questions that do not lead Topi. You may think there is little to talk about, but Topi might see it differently. There may be areas where Topi is delighted to be seen as average, having worked hard to plug a skills gap, or there might be competences that Topi would like to develop into real strengths.

Asking questions like *"People seem to see you as a good all rounder. How do you feel about that?"* can help you begin to pick apart the report and begin a meaningful conversation. Even simple questions like *"What parts of your role do you enjoy the most?"* can start a conversation that will help Topi think about where she would like to excel. You might find yourself discussing roles that Topi could move into to give her a chance to shine, or projects Topi could suggest to stretch herself.

You might discover how Topi would like to shape her skills in the future and be able to come up with some helpful action points. Alternatively, Topi might be very content where she is. Sometimes Topi has no work based aspirations and just wants a pay packet at the end of the month. You may have heard of workers like this referred to as foot soldiers or steadies. Most organisations need them; it's not possible for all of us to rise to the top, and many places of work need people capable of mundane tasks with little hope of promotion.

Finding development points in this situation can be a challenge. If you try too hard Topi will probably tune out. Better to be led by Topi and hopefully identify a couple of small areas of interest or tasks that she will commit to. She may end up with a simpler development plan than others, but we can't expect everyone to sign up for the same level of development activity.

8.4 What do I do when Topi is really disliked?

If you are faced with a report about someone who seems truly unpopular, firstly double check your own body language and make sure you are not portraying yourself as tense or expecting a difficult time. You'll be discussing sensitive issues, so you need to do your very best to create an environment where Topi can open up and discuss delicate issues.

It is possible that Topi is disliked just because she isn't very good at her job and that impacts on those around her. When this is the case, it's not too complicated. You may need to help Topi recognise how her actions affect her colleagues; it's remarkable how often people don't think this through. The Perceptual Positions exercise above in the section on exploring may help here. If Topi has skills gaps, the route forward will either be development, or performance management.

Unfortunately, it is often not a simple case of Topi not doing a job well. If she is really disliked, the underlying reasons are more likely to be about her behaviour and how she displays negative aspects of her personality. How much progress you can make depends on how willing Topi is to change. You might find that she is initially very defensive, but often she is able to look at the report honestly once she is over her initial emotional reaction.

My view is that there are two jobs to be done here before you can begin talking about ways forward. The first is to help Topi paint a picture of her preferred scenario. How does she want people to respond to her? What does she want the atmosphere to be like at work? How would she like to be treated by others, including her boss and team mates? Spend some time exploring so that Topi builds up a convincing image in her mind of how she wants the future to be. One advantage of this exercise is that it is very positive, so it can help prevent you both being dragged into focusing on the bad stuff.

Once you have done this, your second task is to pinpoint some of the key behaviours that are causing issues, and the contexts in which they occur. Topi might be able to explain why she acts as she does in some situations – after all, it is learned behaviour from somewhere. What is 'acceptable' behaviour varies a great deal from family to family and company to company. From here, you can:

- Help her identify different ways of behaving in certain contexts. Generate some options. Don't tell her how to behave – help her explore the alternatives and only fill the gaps if she really struggles.
- Go through the options and explore how others might respond. Topi might need some prompting here, if she is unused to thinking from the other person's perspective. You are looking for the option that will take her closest to the desired outcome she has already identified.
- Talk through what it would take to move her from where she is now to being comfortable using the desired behaviour.

Here's a true story that illustrates this process. Lorraine told me she felt dragged down by the amount of negativity in the office. A little exploring revealed that whinging and sniping tended to occur around the water cooler, and that Lorraine took part in the conversations she didn't like. At first, she couldn't see any other option. With a little prompting, she came up with:

- Walking away
- Turning the conversation to something more positive
- Asking her colleagues to stop being negative

Lorraine realised that just walking away might not get the solution she wanted, but it was a good place to start. We talked through how she might approach the other options to give her the confidence to try them.

Right at the start we talked about knowing your boundaries. If this type of conversation takes you out of your skills set, be honest with Topi and be prepared to discuss who else can help her. It may be that she will need to seek support from a coach or mentor to help her embed new behaviours.

A couple of final points: if you tell someone to stop a behaviour, but they don't have a replacement behaviour anywhere in their knowledge or experience, you are asking for the impossible. Make sure Topi recognises that other behaviours are available, even if she doesn't know yet how to incorporate them into her life.

Lastly, don't be despondent if Topi seems intransigent. I've had a couple of clients who appeared immovable. They were right, everyone else was wrong, they didn't have a problem, and everyone else did. They didn't seem to take anything I said on board at all. Yet the seeds were sown. In both cases, they went away and realised that actually, they did want things to be different. Both came to me with whispers that they were about to be sacked; both were promoted within months. Lorraine was one of them.

8.5 What do I do when Topi is a superstar?

It's great to see a report with high scores and glowing comments all over it – but how on earth do you find development points? It's not always easy when it appears that Topi is at the top of her game. Your conversation might be at a higher level and more future focused here. Topi is obviously an asset, so one way forward might be to ask her how the organisation can maximise her contribution. Topi may be happy in her current role, or she might be wanting to stretch her wings; helping her to think through how she wants her career to develop could be useful.

One danger is that Topi could get bored in her current role as it presents few challenges. It is worth asking her how he feels about her current position – she may not have thought about it, but it makes sense to tackle it before Topi gets jaded and her performance starts to slide. Don't assume, though, that Topi wants to further her career. Like the Steadies above, there are some folk who are happy to stay in a role they excel at and won't be budged!

It's also useful to help Topi pick apart which of her strengths she enjoys using the most. We learn quickest when we're tuning in to things that come naturally to us and we enjoy, so a discussion around how Topi can build on her strengths might prove fruitful. Another angle might be drivers – what is it that makes Topi successful at all she does? What motivates her? Are there any potential dangers that could cause her success levels to drift?

Lastly, it's probable that Topi's colleagues don't all shine as brightly as she does. A very interesting conversation would be to ask Topi how she could help others achieve her standards.

You might then be able to come up with development points which are around coaching or supporting others.

8.6 What do I do when I know there are no promotion prospects?

Firstly, remember that it's not your fault! You can't be held responsible for your company's structure or the economy. There is a danger, though, that when discussing a 360 report, the conversation turns to next steps, which for many understandably includes thinking about promotion.

It may not be an issue for Topi, but if it is, be careful to phrase your words carefully to emphasise that promotion within the company may be an option, but it may not. There might be solid facts you can refer to, for example there may be a current freeze on hiring. There are a couple of useful conversations to have; one is around identifying the skills Topi can develop to put her in the best possible position to grab any opening that does come her way. You can look for opportunities within your organisation to stretch her – for example special projects or responsibilities – that will not only help her develop skills, but will also get her known by more people, which is always useful.

Secondly, you could deal with it head on and ask Topi directly how she feels about the lack of promotion opportunities in the company. Topi might not have thought about this before, or articulated it, but her views can be useful information when it comes to choosing action points. Topi might not embrace the lack of prospects, but it is better to be honest with her than build up false expectations which will cause Topi to lose faith in you.

8.7 What do I do when we don't have enough development opportunities?

For me, there is nothing worse than seeing Topi fired up with a new sense of direction and a lengthy development plan including all sorts of expensive courses, coupled with an unrealistic expectation that the company will stump up all the budget required. There will always be some training that companies will pay for, and plenty they won't. They will also always be looking for more cost effective ways of getting results. The chances are that you won't actually know in detail what can be funded.

You might find yourself walking a narrow plank between encouraging Topi to come up with development ideas and tempering her enthusiasm so that she doesn't get too carried away. My approach is try to instil in Topi the notion (if it isn't there already) that personal development is her responsibility – after all, the skills remain with Topi wherever she goes in the future. If the company is prepared to provide training, coaching or any other type of support, it is a bonus and not an automatic right.

If your discussion brings up areas where Topi would like to learn new skills or improve existing ones, encourage her to think of a few options for achieving each one. You'll want to take into account how she prefers to learn, and also her own time and energy resources. Sometimes you can come up with solutions that utilise 'dead' time, for example listening to podcasts while driving, or watching videos on the train. The idea is that if the company cannot provide the training Topi wants, she has other options for reaching her goals.

8.8 What do I do if Topi gets emotional and irrational?

This really doesn't happen often. Topi can get quite nervous, both at the prospect of receiving a 360 report, and also spending time with you, as she may feel she is going to be confronted with things she would rather avoid. Ninety per cent of the time, Topi's nerves will recede to manageable proportions if you explain what is going to happen and your role well at the beginning – it sets her at ease – which is one reason why contracting (see the skills section above) is so important.

Be observant for clues to Topi's mood. If she continues to seem anxious, you have two choices: you can either continue to reassure her by carrying out the meeting in your usual friendly yet professional manner, in the hope that she will eventually relax into it, or you can take the bull by the horns and tell her what you see *"Topi, you seem a bit anxious today. Is there anything we should talk about before we carry on with this?"*

You will be the judge of which approach to try. You will need to establish whether it is sensible to continue. There is little point if Topi is not able to play her part in the meeting. You may not even know if the anxiety (or whatever emotion you see) is the result of facing the 360 report, something else going on in her life in the moment, or just how she usually is.

I'd say it's okay to continue if Topi seems a bit anxious but is contributing to the discussion. If, however, she seems completely distracted and is only giving minimal input, you could be wasting your time. I'd be inclined to gently ask her what is on her mind.

If somewhere along the way you encounter an outburst, beware of your response to it. You might feel defensive if Topi is angry, or go into rescuing mode if Topi is weepy. Try not to get drawn into the drama but instead hold your supportive composure and let Topi get it out of her system (unless she is being abusive or scaring you, in which case, leave). When Topi has calmed down, you can sensitively ask what the trigger was that caused the outburst. Depending on how serious you assess the situation to be, you can ask her whether she wants to continue. If she is unsure, offer her a drink to give her time to compose herself and then suggest you give it a try. You can ask her if she is happy to continue after a few minutes if you are still not sure how she is coping.

Don't be afraid to cut the meeting short if you are getting nowhere.

8.9 What do I do when Topi doesn't want to speak to me?

On rare occasions, Topi isn't very grown up and takes the seemingly childish approach of not engaging with you. We can only guess why she would choose to do this, but likely reasons are:

- She doesn't want to discuss personal things with you. Who are you anyway?
- She expects the meeting to be a waste of time
- She thinks that the less she says, the less tasks she'll get on her action plan
- She thinks it's the quickest way to get out of the room
- She is painfully shy

Looking at the list, you'll be able to see that with the exception of shyness (in which case you just need to go slowly and sensitively to win Topi's trust), the others could all be addressed with a healthy dose of contracting at the beginning of the meeting. Your problems only begin if Topi makes all the right noises during the first few minutes and then refuses to engage once you get to the meat of the report. Should you continue? Or not? Every situation is different and you will need to make a judgement call.

My option would be to use what counsellors call immediacy. This means stopping doing whatever you had planned to discuss, and instead ask Topi what is going on between the two of you. *"Topi, you agreed to look at this section with me, yet you're not really engaging in conversation. This makes it hard for me to continue. Can we talk about what is going on?"* There are some techniques for challenging Topi in the skills section above which can help. In essence, you are asking a direct question that is difficult for Topi to avoid, but you will use a gentle 'I'm curious' manner so that Topi is not antagonised.

If you're not sure to what degree Topi is taking the report on board, ask her some searching questions to help you find out, e.g. *"Topi, what would you say the top points of this section are?"* *"What is the main thing you'll take from this section?"* Her replies – or lack of them – will help you assess whether it is worth continuing.

The other person involved

8.10 What do I do when the report seems contradictory?

Humans are very complex beings. We are quite capable of acting in contradictory ways. Sometimes just the culture of the groups we find ourselves in is diverse and we adapt accordingly. It might be that in one branch office, everyone is sociable, talkative and informal, so Topi is the same to fit in. Another branch might have a more 'heads down, get on with it, keep yourself to yourself' culture – so Topi does that when she works there. Sometimes we act differently with those higher up the tree to us than those beneath us, or have differing relationships with different departments.

Sometimes we are aware that we behave differently, but often it is a subconscious response. The main thing is not to worry about it. It does not mean the report is 'wrong' – after all, it is only other people's perceptions, we all see through our own lenses.

It is possible that Topi is initially confused by the apparent contradictions, so you may need to reassure her that it is quite common, and that you will be working together to make sense of it. From there, it is a case of taking each section and making sure you get Topi to consider where the perceptions are coming from. Either she might present herself differently according to the situation, or it might be about the perceptions of others.

Think of it as pieces of a jigsaw if it helps, but on the other hand, don't expect all the pieces to fall into place perfectly. Neither you nor Topi will be able to explain completely what was going through others' minds when they answered the questionnaire.

8.11 What do I do when Topi won't accept the feedback?

Sometimes Topi has spent years building very strong defences against the world and doesn't take kindly to anyone suggesting that she do things differently. If you start to sense that this is the case, reinforce that the report is other people's perceptions based on their experience of Topi, which isn't the same as fact. However, if many people score Topi the same way, there is a reason for them all agreeing.

You can't make Topi accept the feedback, but you can ask her to consider it thoughtfully. Remain good humoured; if Topi senses a standoff she is likely to continue to be entrenched in her views. One method that may prove helpful is a gap analysis. Ask her how she sees reality compared to what the report is suggesting, identify the difference and ask her to think about why the gap might exist – what are people seeing? How are they experiencing her and her work?

Another technique you could try is asking her what she would do in your shoes. You could even try all the perceptual positions and ask what someone observing your conversation might think. Some of the techniques in the skills section above on challenging might help too. Ultimately, you have kept your half of the bargain and can only hope that over time Topi softens and takes the report on board.

8.12 What do I do when Topi fixates on the negative?

Many of us are programmed to focus on the bad. Many a time I've seen Topi try to skip over the good bits so that she can concentrate on the lowest scores; I guess many of us have become conditioned to try and fix things that are wrong.

We've already mentioned that if it's possible, try to get Topi to look at the overview before you get to the detail. If from there she is keen to look at the lower scores, then that's okay, she can choose in which order she addresses things. The challenge to be overcome is to move her on from there to get a balanced view of the whole report.

You could start by acknowledging that you understand that Topi wants to look at the down side first – this of course implies that there is a second and third to be looked at – so you are planting the seed that the job is incomplete. You can also make it clear that this section is dealt with; you can ask Topi to summarise her thoughts and ideas for actions to address the section which should give a signal that it's time to move on.

If Topi doesn't respond to the 'moving on' cues, you may need to be a bit firmer with her. *"Topi, you were very keen to look at the low scores, but you don't seem so enthusiastic to look at the other areas. Can you explain that to me?"* *"We've identified your development points, Topi. Let's move on now to look at your strengths. When would you say you are at your best?"*

Don't be afraid to tell Topi that she does not appear to be taking a balanced view, and that she is overlooking her strengths. You can explain to her that working on our strengths can be more productive than working on our weaknesses, because we get more progress for our effort.

Read up on strengths if you are not familiar with the theory *(Now Discover Your Strengths, Marcus Buckingham)*. If she is struggling, give her your summation of the report, using the overview to back up your interpretation.

Topi may not be used to hearing positive feedback, so take extra care to make sure she does not dismiss it.

8.13 What do I do when Topi has a low scoring report?

It can be soul destroying to have a 360 report where all the scores are below average; the implication is that Topi is not good enough to do her job. She is unlikely to be happy about this and it gives you a difficult task. It might be useful, once you have looked at the overview, to ask Topi whether her results are as she expected or if there are surprises. This can give you a handle on her self awareness.

You can also ask if she thinks there are reasons for the low scores. It may be that she has had her role changed frequently, she has been off sick, or she is in the wrong role. It's worth establishing early on if she has an explanation. Whether she is right or wrong, at least it gives you a starting point to explore.

Make it clear to Topi that now she has this information, difficult though it is, she has the opportunity now to plan to improve the situation. It's also worth finding out if she wants to keep her job or whether she would rather find a better match for her skills, so that you can adapt your conversation accordingly.

Another useful strategy can be to ask Topi to identify the top three areas where improvement would make a real difference. This can bring a sense of perspective by making progress seem manageable rather than overwhelming.

Even if Topi seems to cope well during the meeting with you, it's quite possible that she will become despondent afterwards. Do what you can to help her find ongoing support to reach her goals.

The Bottom Line

I hope this book helps you give effective 360 feedback, and that the tools and strategies in it help you on your way. It's based on my own experiences, you'll learn your own as you go along. You'll probably learn as much about yourself as Topi does about herself along the way.

360 feedback should be a positive experience. Afterwards, Topi should be more self aware, more confident about her strengths and have plans in place to help her reach her goals. The bottom line is that in some way, Topi should be further forward than she was before – and that is your benchmark. The end result is hopefully that Topi is a better employee.

Bibliography

Buckingham, Marcus **Now Discover Your Strengths** Gallup Press 2013

Cooper, Julie **Face to Face in the Workplace** Spring Publishing 2012

Cooper, Julie and Reynolds, Ann **The One to One Toolkit 2nd Edition** Careertrain Publishing 2013

De Bono, Edward **Six Thinking Hats** Penguin 2009

Have you enjoyed this book?

If so, please do leave a review. Even a sentence will do, it just helps others to know what to expect. You can either email it directly to us, and we can include it on the Spring Publishing website. Alternatively, you can leave it at Amazon, or anywhere else readers will find it.

If you would like some help training your staff to discuss 360 feedback, do let me know. julie@springdevelopment.net

Keep in touch! Please do join our People Tips mailing list at www.springdevelopment.net for practical guidance on getting the best out of others.

About the Author

Julie Cooper

Hello. I'm a trainer, coach and author specialising in one to one skills. I have a background in advice and guidance, which no doubt has influenced my approach to discussing 360 feedback. I understand that busy people want accessible, practical information. They rarely have time or inclination to read complicated tomes, which is why my books are packed with instantly usable techniques and tips.

Please do check out my company, Spring Development which offers training and development to organisations and individuals that want to flourish and get the best out of their working lives. I've worked with many companies in different sectors – the only common denominator being that they want their people to succeed. If you are in the UK, I'd be happy to talk to you about developing your people.

I'm based in a village near Banbury in Oxfordshire, so ideally placed for reaching most places easily. Outside of work, I enjoy looking after my newly inherited amazingly beautiful garden, exploring The Cotswolds, and seeking out live music, arts and crafts.

Other Books By Julie Cooper:

Face to Face in the Workplace: A handbook of Strategies for Effective Discussions ISBN 978-0955968037

Looking to improve your management skills? This is an accessible guide to every meeting, discussion or difficult conversation you will need to have.

Written for busy people who need quick solutions, Face to Face in the Workplace will equip you with all the tools and strategies you'll need to get it right every time.

Step by step frameworks will guide you in getting the best out of the people you manage, and yourself. You will: have more productive discussions that please everyone involved; save time by knowing how to prepare effectively; never have to worry about what to say in difficult meetings; learn to get your point over more effectively; improve your people management skills – and your career prospects.

Included: Assertive behaviour, Explaining, Listening, Interviewing applicants, Making someone redundant, Saying no, Shutting people up, Introducing change, Self awareness, Dismissing a member of staff, Personality styles, Challenging, Questioning, Credibility, Rapport, Body language, Respect, Appraisals, Return to work interviews, Challenging attitude, Coaching, Feedback, Conflict, The Dark Triad, Negotiating, Delegating, Exit interviews, Instructing, Influencing, Inappropriate behaviour, Managing your boss, Mentoring, Performance gaps, Praising, Supervising, Reprimanding, Supporting through change, 360° feedback.

"This year's Must Have book" HR Director magazine

Co-Authored with Ann Reynolds:

The One to One Toolkit: Tips and Strategies for Advisers, Coaches and Mentors

by Julie Cooper and Ann Reynolds   ISBN 978-0955968051

Does your job involve helping people to move forward in their career, learning, or personal development? If so, this book is for you. It aims to meet the needs of people employed in the field of advice and guidance in a practical, user friendly way.

It explains useful models, suggests strategies for dealing with difficulties, and provides powerful, memorable tools to use with clients.

Part One takes you, step by step, through a tried and trusted model for giving advice, including highlighting dangers and difficulties in a 'how to' manner.

Part Two provides a more in depth model, focusing on guidance, explaining how to help your client in a professional manner when their needs are more complex.

Part Three is The Toolkit – a collection of bite sized theories, tips, exercises and strategies that can be used with clients in a one to one setting. Topics include decision making, changing perception, expanding horizons, positive thinking, learning and coaching. Widely used as a text for organisations training advisers.

"I love this little book. It gives me new guidance ideas every time I open it." **Amazon review**

The Groupwork Toolkit: How To Convert Your One To One Advice Skills To Work With Groups

by Ann Reynolds and Julie Cooper ISBN 978-0955968013

The Groupwork Toolkit makes groupwork easy by showing you how to recognise and transfer the skills you already have.

Advisers, coaches and mentors have a wealth of interpersonal and communication skills, but may lack the experience and confidence to transfer them successfully to running groups. The Groupwork Toolkit can help.

It demystifies groupwork, and gives you the confidence and knowledge you need to facilitate groups, whether your group are learning new skills, or have come for advice or guidance. It explains how you can deliver brilliant groupwork by planning well, setting objectives and using a variety of training techniques.

How people learn is covered, explaining the different ways people learn so you can adapt your style and methods to meet the needs of each group. There is a step by step model for producing a session plan, with plenty of practical tips and activities to use. Sample session plans are also included.

Lastly, sound advice on how to manage a group includes keeping the group involved and interested, and how to handle those difficult situations and individuals. If you need to provide group guidance, deliver career or job search sessions, this is the book for you.

"The Groupwork Tool Kit saved my life when I was doing my groupwork assessment for the QCG". Francesca Hall

The Job Interview Toolkit: Exercises to get you fit for your interview

by Ann Reynolds and Julie Cooper   ISBN 978-0955968020

The Job Interview Toolkit is a practical, easy to follow guide to preparing for interviews, ideal for job seekers of all ages, especially the young and those returning to work after a break.

It contains a selection of activities, organised in the five-step TAPAS programme, designed to get you fit to perform like a star on the day. Its easy to read format make it accessible to job seekers of all ages. Advisers will find ideas for working with their clients too.

This book is:

Easy to read – short sections, illustrations and diagrams, examples and danger stories.

Practical – with things to do, questions to answer, photos to comment on, things to practise with a friend. Most of us learn best by doing, so you will find a five-step programme of exercises to get you fit and ready for the interview (the really important facts are there too).

A simple framework that is easy to learn:T-A-P-A-S. Think – Analyse – Prepare – Adjust – Shine!

This book will make sure you know what to do, perform at your best and sell yourself brilliantly!

"I re-read it before my last interview – and got the job! " **Micky Waycot**